ISBN-13: 9798867952259

Cover design by: Stefan Griess, Micah Hakes
Library of Congress Control Number: 2018675309
Printed in the United States of America

CONTENTS

INTRODUCTION

Very early in my IT career, I would browse the internet trying to find the ideal career path. I wanted something that fit nicely with my interests and my situation. I searched for the best certification. I took the time to read articles on how to land a great job. I wanted to know how to make it happen! I searched the internet for all kinds of ways to appeal to the company that would be the best for me (and pay me the most I could get).

To this day, I am at times searching for the next ideal certification, and the ideal job that will give me the most room to grow. It can be a real struggle to find your way in the IT industry.

Every time I searched I noticed something. Even when I used a variety of descriptive search terms, every article and blog post contained just surface-level how to's. They were all cookie-cutter, surface-level steps—even when I asked ChatGPT!

How to's for an IT career can be somewhat helpful, but I have found them to be over-simplified and not very helpful. It is almost like most of the tech community has tried to solve career problems like technology problems

—with how to's. Don't get me wrong. Verified how-to's for solving technical problems are incredibly helpful. But career paths are not technical issues. Navigating our technology careers with clarity requires mindset modification.

I encourage you to put this book down for a few minutes and test what I've said. Pull out your device and search the internet for IT career advice, and see what you come up with. Everything you find will be essentially just as I described above: basic steps, certification lists, relevant jobs. For example, search your preferred search engine for "how to become a network administrator." The results will be articles outlining only surface-level, generalized steps that you probably already know: get educated, get an internship, get a degree, get a cert, and build your network.

Over-generalized guidance is difficult to apply to our unique situations. It can be pretty discouraging to come away from these articles without any better picture of how to entrench ourselves in the IT industry and set ourselves up for success. The *mental* steps and *mindset* for growing where we are and progressing in our tech careers are nearly undefined. They are mostly 404 - Not Found.

Maybe the career advice offered on the internet is a symptom of our impoverished desires. Perhaps we are satisfied too easily with how to's for our IT career. It is almost as if we approach our careers with the same "just show me how to do it" mentality as we do with tech issues. Do we expect to operate and improve our IT career like we operate and fix technology? It seems safe to say that if we apply a surface-level approach to our careers, it shouldn't surprise us if we aren't that satisfied. We must go deeper.

I think it is *worth* going deeper. Why not get to the heart of our mindset and into the details of our mental steps as we navigate our career? What if we went further and asked for mindset principles? What if we not only asked *how* but also *why* regarding our IT career?

A successful tech career is not less than how-to's. It's just SO much more.

A successful technology career is putting in the mental sweat for the achievement and exhilaration of discovery. It is solving problems with real solutions because it's so awesome to understand why the issue occurred and how to prevent it. Don't you want to know more than just "X problem needs X solution?" Don't you want to know how and why it gets fixed in the way that it does? A successful technology career is being fully engaged in the details and the pursuit of deep knowledge. Don't you want to know how to apply that awesome knowledge to accomplish really cool things?

Let's go beyond the lesser how to's for our IT careers and go much deeper. If we ask more relevant questions about our IT career, I am certain we will get more relevant answers.

What mindset would most drive success in our IT careers?

What kind of mental steps and mindset principles

could we cultivate to enjoy long-term success?

How could we embed these mindset principles into our thought habits and behavior patterns as we go about our daily work?

How do we actualize this mindset right now so we can grow right where we are?

Who This Book is For

For those who are considering transitioning to an IT career, these answers will help you decide your path forward with a little more certainty. If you decide to start a new career in IT, making some mental adjustments and aligning with the mindset principles we will discuss will smoothen your path. To help ease you in, I offer not surface-level tips but deep, refined principles to help make these mental adjustments real. If we want deep satisfaction in our careers, we need deep principles that reach the root of our mindsets so we can make progress in the present. I will help you understand the challenges ahead and help prime you with a mindset to overcome these challenges.

For those who are relatively early in their IT career and have some experience in IT, I will define and explain the mindset principles that make successful IT engineers excel. Internalizing and practicing these mindset principles as you go about your daily work will help you grow right where you are.

For the rest of you who are already successful IT engineers, managers, directors, CIO's, CTO's, etc., . . . read on. I think you will want to get this handbook into the hands of your team members.

Before I jump into these principles and give you what I've promised, let me share my story with you as briefly as I can. It will help you understand where I'm coming from and how these mindset principles can help you.

A LITTLE ORIGIN STORY
AND MY MISSION

In 2008, I finished a B.A. in Philosophy and enrolled into an M.Div. program. By the end of 2009 and right in the middle of the recession, I quit the M.Div. program. But nobody wants to hire a recent college grad with a Philosophy degree in a recession! Literally, no one does. And I get it. Everything I knew up to that point was studying, writing, and test-taking. I had been a full-time student since I was age five. I had no idea what I was doing when it came to building a career. But unfortunately for me I had to go looking for a job in the middle of the Great Recession. Talk about an effort in futility! During my futile search in a recession, I met people with Ph.D.'s and master's degrees who could not land a job at Panera or even McDonald's. It was that bad.

I bounced from job to job, constantly looking for some career that had potential and longevity. Even after I got my first job in IT, I was struggling to stay afloat mentally. I was not feeling successful in my career because learning something so new and complex was difficult. I typically learn quickly and pick things up fairly easily. But I did not develop the necessary troubleshooting skills as quickly because I didn't know how to adjust my mindset for the work. I really, really struggled in this way. I could not get things fixed and resolved as quickly as I wanted to, which led to quite a few doubts about my future in tech. Fixing technical issues did not come naturally to me. It was an uphill climb, and there were quite a few times I was tempted to quit and find something easier. But I had already bounced around to different jobs in quite a few different industries. I did not have any other options; I had to make it work. When the going was very difficult, it was hard to keep going. At some point, something had to give—either my career in IT, or my mindset.

I was working in a department with very well-trained and skilled professionals. They had IT degrees, IT certifications and many years of experience. They had grown up tinkering with technology. Me? I had grown up studying history, the classics, languages like Latin and Greek, and wrote lots of papers. (Wave the white flag and give up now, right?) I had never even had a hobby that included tinkering or fixing things. *None* of IT came naturally to me. I felt like I was trying to pedal uphill on a unicycle. To make an IT career work, I had to learn to ride... or die.

I did not have any other option because I had already tried pretty much every other option! I had worked in retail, heavy equipment, adult foster care, landscaping, security, insurance, sales, warehousing, construction, and on and on. Not only did I not have another option at hand, but I also did not have any other possibility that I could think of that *might* unfold into a career for me. It was truly sink or swim for me. Even after getting my first major certification I made my home computer inoperable. How did I pull that off? By thinking I knew more than I actually did. (This kind of thinking is actually a common pitfall that we will address later in this book!) So please understand that I did not have a leg up with my skills, education or background. I will admit that I did possess one thing—desperation! I had to make it work because I barely had enough for next month's rent!

I could continue to detail my struggles and successes during my first 500 to 1,000 days in IT. But I think you understand the point. It was especially challenging because my mindset had to be modified. My whole way of thinking and working had to undergo forced metamorphosis. Mindset-level changes are never quick or easy.

My goal is to make your mindset modification a bit more clear. I do not want your journey in IT to be as lengthy or difficult as mine was. So I offer you the following principles to cultivate a mindset that catalyzes your technology career and actuates your growth.

MINDSET PRINCIPLE #1: STICK WITH IT

"Oh, great, the same advice all over again," you may be thinking. You have heard this before, and it is getting so old.

Wait! Hold on a minute.

Before you put this book down in disgust at this shameless cliché, will you dive briefly with me into this principle? It will be worth it, I promise. Remember, going deeper with our career mindset will be *worth* it. Possessing this mindset principle will reward you, so stick with me. The rest of the mindset principles and mental tools I share depend on whether this this important principle finds its home in your mindset. You need this mindset principle so you can remain steadfast in response to the challenges in your IT career.

This mindset principle is no cliché when it comes to your technology career. Your day to day experience in the tech space will be demanding sometimes. But if you persist, it truly will pay off. You need a persistent, steadfast mindset that is committed to your career in the tech space. Here are few ways to remain motivated.

We get paid to learn cool things and make the magic of IT happen. Our rewards are those "Aha" moments when we figure a new technology out. The unique exuberance of being able to say "I figured it out and fixed it" is ours when we put in some serious mental sweat, take good risks, and come through with a true solution. It's the persistent ones who know what it really takes to solve tough problems. This singular satisfaction is reserved for those willing to work for it. When we persist through and fix a really tough problem, we gain some serious mental confidence. And confidence produces more results. This is when technology is truly fun. It's an awesome reward, and it feeds our motivation really well.

I encourage you now, wherever you are in your tech career journey, to be as passionately committed to your own growth as possible. This is another way to feed your motivation. Remaining committed to your own growth and focusing on exercising and honing your own skills will catalyze your progress. Doing so helps you grow right where you are, and helps you avoid looking too far ahead. This mindset will help you engage problems and overcome them in the present. Every problem ticket and every challenge are opportunities to grow. Growth in your technical abilities means growth in your earnings and advancement in your career. The tech space is in-demand.

So if you're not being challenged and growing at one company, your skills can help you advance at another.

Remind yourself that working in technology is one of few careers that have a low barrier to entry and a high return on your time and money. This reality is also highly motivating. A career in tech advances you for your earned results and certifications. This is much more attainable, and therefore attractive. It is especially true in IT that your development and advancement is directly related to your work ethic and results. Besides, it can be expensive to pay for a degree both in terms of time and money (even if your employer pays for it). But in the tech space, you do not necessarily need a degree to advance. You just need to know your stuff and demonstrate your proficiency, and certifications accomplish this extremely well. Many employers recognize that tech certifications verify and demonstrate your skills very well. And tech certifications are much more affordable when compared to the price of a degree.

But please do not misunderstand me. A computer science degree or other technology degree *is* valuable for your career. Many companies like both degrees and certifications. And every company likes *experience*. But pursuing a 2-4 year degree is not always practical for each of us. But a couple of certifications can be completed in a year. You can make it work going the certification route if need be. Companies looking for technical talent love technical certifications. And for those needing or wanting to change careers, plenty of employers will appreciate the maturity and experience you have. Just make sure your resume demonstrates your technical and transferrable skills so that you can articulate how you will add value to their company.

It makes sense to commit to a tech career, doesn't it? You can enter this field without a degree by attaining a certification and demonstrating some experience. And your return on investment will be high if you commit to growing your knowledge and skills.

But a "stick-with-it" mindset means more than committing to a tech career. You need to develop a tenacity with your daily work. If you are already working a technical job, resolve problems by staying in attack mode. (If you are not yet in a technology position but are pursuing a degree or cert, do the same. Stay tenacious in the moment with each demo and lab.) Do not give up easily. Let your curiosity overcome your fear of failure. Remind yourself that you will be rewarded. Pursue those rewards by being passionately committed to your own growth. Growth comes by taking courage and attacking and facing these challenges head on.

Steadfast persistence is mindset principle #1 because it is the root mindset from which your tech career can grow. Challenges will come, but this firm persistence is the root of all the following mindset principles we will discuss. Mental persistence and commitment to your own growth will hold you fast while your mind is stretched and your mental muscles are strengthened throughout your career.

I believe you (yes, you who are reading this right now) can do this if you are ready to learn. If you are willing to be coached, if you are okay with some hard knocks, and if you are resilient despite setbacks, you can achieve success in a tech a career. Your mind is a muscle, and you are ready to train and strengthen that muscle. You are committed to learn to your utmost which will help you earn to your utmost. You can go as far as your commitment will take you in this industry because the tech space rewards hard work. Commit to giving yourself time to learn from more experienced team members too.

Give yourself a chance to fail, and then learn from the experience. Every mistake or oversight is a good one, unless you fail to learn from it. So allow yourself the opportunity to learn by trial and error. Be okay with momentary mistakes and temporary failures, acknowledge them, and work to resolve them. If you learn from them as they occur, you will not repeat them in more impactful situations later.

Commit to sharpening your sensitivities with how the devices, platforms, code and technologies work and interact with each other. Take the learner's approach: stay humble and listen.

And finally, understand this: *bosses like hosses*. Don't be half-hearted in your commitment to yourself, your growth, and your work. Be a hoss and embrace every challenge with heart and grit. Approach your career with an attitude that is ready to persist, giddy up, and hoss on.

MINDSET PRINCIPLE #2: CULTIVATE CONSTANT CURIOSITY

Imagine a completely trustworthy, seasoned IT guy with black-rimmed glasses and a salt and pepper goatee saying in a soft, certain voice, "Stay *curious*, my friend."

In IT, we need to *stay curious. Constantly.* Let's take the idea of lifelong learning to the max and be committed to being a sponge. We need to soak up every detail, and stoke up our curiosity's appetite. Be a student of our business. Study our craft. Stay on top of our game. And remain curious.

Like that noble steed, we need to let our curiosity roam wild and free. Let's be excited about understanding problems and discovering solutions. As we gain knowledge and learn new technologies, let's remember to keep asking "how?" and "why?" "Why implement it this way, or another way? How does this piece interact with this other piece of technology? What is the relationship between these components and how do they interact and interoperate?"

Asking questions like these will help us go deep and be comprehensive in our knowledge. We do not want segmented knowledge. We want integrated, holistic knowledge of how things interoperate. If we have only fragmented pieces of knowledge that are scattered and disconnected, what good is that? If we have not put in the work to discover the inner workings of the technologies and tools, we will only be able to poke the big problems, mostly mis-diagnose them, put in shoddy solutions, probably make them worse, and never really figure things out. (Sounds janky, doesn't it!? Because it is!) We're not curious enough if we are making those kinds of mistakes. We do not want to end up being a mile wide but only an inch deep. Let's leverage our curiosity to go deep and understand comprehensively.

The way to implement our curiosity and make it operative is at least three-fold, though these are not exhaustive. First, let's resolve never to be content with having issues just resolved. Of course, it is good to solve problems, close tickets and complete assignments. But if we never figure out *why* a problem got solved or never learn *how* a particular solution addressed the issue, we are not developing and maintaining a growth mindset. If we follow this path, we are too easily satisfied. Only knowing that X solution fixes X problem and that Y solution fixes

Y problem doesn't help us grow and deepen our expertise. If we never ask how and why, we will never go deep enough and we will stagnate our growth. We want to be proactive and know how to prevent the issue in the future, right? Let's not let our relief at the resolution outweigh our curiosity for knowing exactly why the issue happened, and how the solution resolved the problem.

Second, let's dive into the details. The proof of our curiosity is wanting to know how things work. If we want to work in technology, we need to figure technology out, understand its terms and technicalities, and improve how it operates. Let's be passionate about how the components operate within their context and how they contribute to the technology's purpose.

Third, let's welcome the problem and the person who reports it. Problems are opportunities to cultivate our curiosity and accelerate our growth. That problem or ticket is simply our next opportunity to advance our knowledge and technical skills. It will require work, but our mental sweat to formulate and apply a real solution will reward us with growth. Our growth will be catalyzed by our constant curiosity. If an issue continues to arise, employees need to be encouraged to voice their concerns and tech problems. We need to be honest about the tech problems that our people face.

We can take this a step further. It's important to discover the problem behind the problem. Problems sometimes cause other problems. Sometimes we're only aware of the surface symptom and unaware of the root problem. We must also understand the impact the problem is having on the business and the people. People will report a small problem, but that problem is a smaller component of a larger technical or business problem. Let's be aware of this and seek to uncover whether there is a larger issue in play. It's wise to take our cues not only from the people, but also from the processes and technology that are part of the issue.

Additionally, we need to take the time to uncover the need behind the need when interfacing with people. At times a deeper business need has not been uncovered. It's important to keep that possibility on our radar and take a consultative approach to understanding the business. Sometimes the deeper need is simply improving the overall process and preventing the issue from ever happening again. Not every issue can be improved to the level of full prevention, but we must at least ensure that we go that far in our consideration of the problem. An ounce of prevention is always worth a pound of cure in IT.

If you have not realized this already, you will as your IT career unfolds: some problems are more complex than others, and not every issue is as it seems. You may face some very complex problems that resist all your best at-hand resolutions. Not everything is always straightforward. It takes time to diagnose new problems accurately. For this reason, we need to be passionately committed to understanding the whole problem   and its context to compose the most sustainable and non-intrusive solution. Implementing a solution that causes or eventually will cause another problem is not a solution.

The kind of curiosity that is fueled by our own uncertainty is what we are after. So let's get mentally prepared to stay persistent in our pursuit of actual solutions. This mindset principle is the foundation for the following four mindset principles focused specifically on troubleshooting. A persistent curiosity will carry us through the challenges of troubleshooting.

MINDSET PRINCIPLE #3: BE BEHAVIOR-FOCUSED IN YOUR ANALYSIS AND TROUBLESHOOTING

When we face a new tech issue, our best option is to discover how that problematic device and technology *is behaving*. It's important to focus on the problematic *behavior* of the issue, and not just the problem it's presenting.

Devices think? Technologies behave? Essentially, yes. Sometimes end users will express out of frustration, "Ugh, those things have a mind of their own." In this they speak truth (much more than they realize).

In fact, they are quite correct. Each device, network, and software has been engineered to behave in a certain way. Each technology is built to execute a particular function, and each is built to interoperate with other technologies. Like people, technologies have certain expectations of each other as they communicate. We need to remain curious to get a sense for how each technology operates in relation to the other technologies it talks with.

It's wise to ask ourselves these kinds of questions as we figure out the problematic behavior:

At what point in the process is this problem occurring?

What is the device and/or software doing at this point that might be part of or contributing to the problem?

Is this component a cause of the problem, or is it just a symptom caused by a different issue that could be the root of the problem?

What is the technology trying to accomplish at the time that the problem occurs?

What was the overall business process and technology built to do?

What might it be expecting that it's not receiving?

What other technologies does it depend on?

As we seek to understand each technology, we need to avoid wandering too far afield. It's best to be conscientious by digging into the details without getting lost in them. We need to try to keep the problem and its behavior in focus as we research various solutions. Let's be as perceptive as possible, and allow ourselves time to analyze the dysfunction and think extensively about the problem. Try to take notice of its behavior in all its details. Its problematic symptoms will typically lead us to a solution if we can pick up on the clues it may be dropping. Other times the issue may be generic and thus more difficult to dig into. Even in this scenario, analyzing the behavior will help us clarify how to proceed.

The reason why we need to analyze the behavior of the issue is to focus our attention away from the surface-level error. Analyzing the behavior will give us the leverage we need to ask the right questions we listed above and get to the bottom of the behavior. Taking this approach will prevent us from fixating on the error or problem itself and get us digging right away into the sub-level causes. We don't want to float among and stay around the surface-level symptoms. We need to get to the root of the issue, and a behavior analysis approach really helps in this regard.

Additionally, analyzing the behavior of the problem will help us get the context of the problem fully in view. It will also stoke our curiosity so that we are sufficiently motivated to continue gathering details. When it comes to technology, there is always a context to be understood. Context always helps define behavior, and vice versa.

Finally, analyzing the behavior helps us compare what the technology is doing vs. what it's supposed to be doing. Our job as technologists is to make things function well. Behavior analysis focuses our attention on function and its context rather than fixating on the issue. Analyzing the underlying technology's behavior gets us beyond the surface and into understanding what is functioning and what isn't.

MINDSET PRINCIPLE #4: BE DETAIL-SENSITIVE AND EXACT IN YOUR TROUBLESHOOTING

Do you know what a paradox is? A paradox is an apparent, but not an actual contradiction. It seems contradictory, but really isn't. To implement this mindset principle, we must be specific and exact in our troubleshooting, yet we must start with the basics. The fundamentals—the first mental steps that we take during our troubleshooting process—define how quickly and thoroughly we'll be able to resolve the issue. Beginning with the fundamentals allows us to cast as wide a net as possible and account for what we don't know or aren't aware of yet. Starting with the basics also allows us to confirm whether we are headed in the right direction. To be able to home in on the specifics and discover the true source of the problem, we will need to start by getting answers to simpler, more basic questions. These questions may seem incredibly basic, but they're very important. Because it is easy to forget how important getting these answers is, we will need to be committed to asking these questions.

This saying still holds true today: "Give someone a fish, and you feed them for a day. But teach them to fish, and you feed them for a lifetime."

Getting answers to these fundamental questions will help us begin to fish (troubleshoot and solve problems) over the lifetime of your IT career:

When did the problem start? And for how long has the issue been occurring? This will help us get a feel for the timing of the issue and can help identify concurrent issues that may also be factors. As they sometimes say, timing is everything. This is very true when it comes to troubleshooting technology.

How many people are experiencing the same issue? It is best to get firm details from people in the same department or from those who perform the same function. They typically will be able to provide additional info, and might be experiencing the same issue. If others perform the same business process regularly, are they experiencing the same issue? If only one person is experiencing the issue—what's unique about this person's technology?

How often and at what point in the business process does the issue occur? Ascertaining the scope of the problem will help us ascertain the issues' frequency. Does the issue happen only once, or every time they execute a specific process?

What is the impact of the problem on the business? If this problem does not get resolved in two hours, what will happen with the business? If not resolved in four hours or even a day, will they be prevented from completing a critical task? Some business processes are mission critical, while others are less important. Answers to these questions will help us place the problem into its context and understand the big picture of what is at stake for the business and the urgency to be assigned.

To sum it up, what we are after in these questions are:

1. Timing
2. Scope
3. Frequency
4. Impact

The examples above are sample questions to help us get relevant answers in the beginning of the troubleshooting process. As we define the Timing, Scope, Frequency and Impact of each problem, patterns and trends will crystallize. Recognizing patterns and trends is so important to our troubleshooting process. We want to troubleshoot and resolve problems so well that we prevent the problem from ever occurring again. Recognizing trends helps us be preventative, and positions us to adjust nimbly to whatever additional challenges arise.

Sometimes it is difficult to get an accurate or clear answer to these questions. Sometimes it is worth clarifying, even asking the same question again to the same person over an extended period of time to verify our understanding. Although it may seem unnecessary, asking the same question again can help ensure we are getting accurate, consistent answers to these questions. We may even get further information that was not available originally. This additional information may prove vital and end up leading to a final resolution.

At other times the issue does not behave consistently, making it even more difficult to get a clear picture of what is happening. But as we work on the problem, let's keep the answers we've received top of mind to maintain our focus and keep us on track. Continuing to ask these questions consistently during troubleshooting will heighten our sensitivity to detail. The more accurate we can be in our understanding of the issue, the more exact we will be in applying the best solution.

By starting with these questions, we will have the information to formulate a *sound, permanent* resolution. It may be tempting to stay satisfied with a temporary solution, or a long-term workaround that seems good enough. Although those kinds of solutions function well as a temporary workaround, if we allow those kinds of solutions to stick around it is likely that another problem may be occasioned or caused directly by this temporary solution.

It is reasonable to want to get the problem resolved quickly. But the key here is to avoid letting our urgency turn into desperation. We cannot allow the relief of a temporary solution to chase us into a corner and keep us hostage to that temporary solution. Temporary solutions only stop the symptom and do not fix the root cause, leaving a higher probability that another issue could arise if the root of the issue remains unresolved. We need to formulate a sound, permanent solution that will resolve the root of the issue. Doing so will minimize future issues for the technology itself, and for the other technologies that touch it.

Over the next few chapters, we will discuss in greater detail how to resolve problems at their root.

MINDSET PRINCIPLE #5: TROUBLESHOOT CREATIVELY

As with most disciplines, the most skilled are those who "have it down to a science." At the same time, their accomplishments are truly "works of art." They make the hard things look easy. The field of technology is no different. The best in IT are both scientific practitioners *and* creative artisans.

But when we are starting out in this field, every technology seems so complex and hard to grasp. If we are honest with ourselves, we are far from being skilled artisans when we are starting out. We are just trying to understand the fundamentals. The challenge is that these technologies are very complex. If we haven't already, we eventually will realize that these technology components only function well under very specific settings and conditions. And all the specifics are incredibly detailed. It's easy to feel overwhelmed at first.

Despite the overwhelming details, be encouraged. If we are putting into practice the previous four mindset principles, we are well-prepared to start implementing this fifth mindset principle. Even though we may be new to the field, we can troubleshoot creatively.

How?

As best we can, we must get ourselves squarely in front of the problem we are trying to solve. If we are trying to solve a problem that is already impacting the business, establish a remote session with the employee and make them demonstrate how the issue occurs. If we cannot remote in with the employee to get in front of the problem, arrange to go to where they are. Don't assume that the issue is exactly as they described or that they've reported a complete picture of the issue. We *must see* what they are experiencing.

We cannot rely on second-hand descriptions, even if those reporting the issue are eyewitnesses. We need to gather the evidence for ourselves and see if from our tech-informed perspective. Their descriptions of the issue are helpful, but they have only one angle on the issue. They understand relatively little about the technology that operates below the surface. But they do know how it normally works. And they can give us some great detail on *when it started, how many people are experiencing it, and what the issue's impact is* (Mindset Principle #4, anyone?).

Once we are in front of the issue with them, let's

do whatever it takes to get screenshots of the steps that precipitate the issue and the issue itself. We need to record what is happening to give ourselves a clear picture of the situation. We want concrete details to take back with us and for our team if the issue is urgent and needs quick escalation.

At this point you are probably wondering, "How does this constitute troubleshooting *creatively*?"

Let's think of ourselves as artists and the screenshots as our paint. With our screenshots, we are building our palette to paint the full picture. Additionally, let's think of ourselves as avid puzzlers who likes to piece together 1,000-piece puzzles. We want to make sure we have all the pieces to the puzzle, and all the colors on our palette to paint a complete resemblance. As technologists, we want to become to the most effective painter-puzzlers we can possibly be. Having that picture clearly in front of us and putting the pieces together is what the troubleshooting process is all about.

We can set up our canvas or our puzzle table, so to speak, by setting up the same environment in which the problem occurs. We need to re-create the circumstances. This means we are going to set up the same type of situation and settings from where the end user is experiencing the problem. We want to piece together the issue right in front of us. Just as we cannot paint a picture or piece together a puzzle when we are even slightly removed from the canvas or table, we cannot troubleshoot effectively when we are distant from the issue. We must do everything we can to get squarely in front of what we are attempting to fix. This will give us the opportunity to grasp the problem's details and context. By doing this, we give ourselves the chance to piece together the root problem in a controlled environment that minimizes unintended consequences to the user environment or business. This is the ideal situation in which issues can be solved at their root with the least amount of risk.

When we encounter an issue that is not easily resolved, getting this environment set up is always worthwhile. We may find that it even took longer to set up the environment than it did to identify the problem and fix it. That's okay, this process was still incredibly worthwhile. And would we have solved it as thoroughly without setting up the same environment? Likely not. And we gained a much greater understanding regarding the technology's details and familiarized ourselves with how it supports the business. We also were able to get to the root of the issue. Yee-haw! Let's keep that troubleshooting environment prepared and handy. If the next issue is more complex, that environment is ready to go and will give us a head start to re-creating the next issue and getting to the root of the issue as fast as possible.

Up to this point with this mindset principle, we have discussed how to think of ourselves as painter-puzzlers. And we have also explored what it looks like to implement this mindset when it comes to troubleshooting. But before we leave this mindset principle to focus on the next one, let's take a closer look at this creative mindset itself and how to cultivate it.

Your own creativity is your secret sauce to resolving technical problems. That problem that simply won't go away and refuses to be fixed might just be needing your unique approach and a fresh perspective. This does not mean that your creative solutions need to be complex. Many times the best solutions are also very simple. But when you are stumped and the issue seems insurmountable, find new angles or take a new approach. Step back so you can get a broader perspective on the problem. Approaching the problem from a different angle will help you not only see the problem in a new way or in new terms, but this will help you cultivate a nimble, creative mindset. Seeking a different angle will help you avoid losing the forest for the trees, so to speak. Finding a fresh perspective will help you avoid getting overwhelmed by the details. And it may help you discover the importance of other components that are contributing to the problem you're trying to resolve.

Remind yourself during your troubleshooting process that you do not have full visibility and that you have much to discover. None of us has a comprehensive understanding of any situation. Although we want to be as comprehensive as possible, we humans always have blindspots. And technologies always present some gotcha's. There is *always* room to grow more deeply and comprehensively in our knowledge. Even when we think we know much, we still have much to discover.

At times we also need to admit to ourselves where

we may be denying a significant source of the problem. We must be willing to recognize when we have eliminated a distinctly probable cause because of our over-confidence instead of honestly dealing with the details. Sometimes we like to eliminate a possible solution because we don't want to admit that that possibility could be the source, or even might be a contributor to the problem. We must try to be aware of how our minds avoid the actual root of the problem when we want to pursue less relevant paths of lesser resistance. Other times we try to avoid admitting a deeper problem lest our own image of success is challenged and called into question. These least-resistant paths develop from not wanting to admit fault, not wanting our self-perception of excellence to be challenged, not wanting to rip off short-term bandage solutions, or not wanting to see our own half-baked solution exposed. These are our mental blind spots, and they inhibit real troubleshooting. If we're denying something that's quietly nagging us, chances are high that we're also too certain about its unworthiness. We must avoid an uber-certainty that can sometimes make us refuse to listen to what the broken technology is trying to tell us. We must be willing to investigate with a healthy dose of self-honesty. Adopting a humble mindset and inspecting the problem with self-honesty often will lead to the long-term solution we really need.

To counteract these blind spots, we should allow all items within the scope of possibility a seat at our troubleshooting table. Sometimes this means we will reluctantly have to learn more about a technology that frankly we are sick of troubleshooting and learning. Other times we will have to admit to ourselves that a previous solution is not as sustainable or permanent as we would like to think. Or it may require us to admit that our implementation of a solution is not as pristine and polished as we would like to think. We don't want to remain in denial just because want false security in our certainty. It's wise to be cautious about what we *think* we know for sure.

Many of us in IT like to fancy ourselves as supreme engineers who only implement the most refined and perfectly configured solutions. But quite often this is not the case; and the problems caused by our implementations are almost always there to remind us. Long-term solutions always require mental sweat, and it takes the most nimble and honest mindset to formulate and implement a truly seamless solution. We're at our best when we maintain nimbleness by seeking new angles to the root of the problem. We can cultivate honesty by willingly seeing and admitting to the weaknesses of our imperfect solutions. Our nimbleness and honesty will be able to turn challenges into major growth opportunities for ourselves.

Remember Mindset Principle #2? One of the most effective ways to prevent over-certainty and avoid implementing measures that don't actually resolve the problem is to balance our urgency with curiosity. When we feel overwhelmed with getting something fixed quickly, our minds are going to try to gain certainty by using confirmation bias. We will assure ourselves that what we *think* we know is true. Our minds are going to try to trick us into satisfying our own mental standards and talk ourselves into a more at-hand resolution rather a solution rooted in reality. As a countermeasure, let's let our curiosity have a seat at the table as we go about inspecting our certainties and finding solutions. This undercurrent of curiosity will help manage the stress and help us implement a real solution. To seek new angles and approach the problem creatively, stay curious just as we discussed in Mindset Principle #2.

Take a few minutes and recall the most impactful recommendations from the mindset principles we've discussed so far. They all build upon each other, each working to launch us further into success. With these mindset principles organized like tools in your mental toolbox, you are ready to dive deeply into Mindset Principle #6.

MINDSET PRINCIPLE #6: RESOLVE PROBLEMS AT THEIR ROOT: BE SURGICAL

In the previous chapter we briefly mentioned getting to the root of the problem. If you think back to Mindset Principle #5, you may remember that I described the mindset required to troubleshoot creatively. Nimbleness, honesty, setting up a test environment, and being a painter-puzzler are all critical components of the mindset we are building. Implementing Mindset Principle #5 puts you in prime position for resolving problems at their root and putting Mindset Principle #6 into practice.

When it comes to resolving problems at their root, we first need to identify a *temporary workaround* for issues that require further troubleshooting. If a real resolution does not surface or come quickly enough, we should implement a temporary mitigation to alleviate the issue for the user(s). A temporary workaround will give us time to find a real, long-term solution.

Above all, avoid reacting quickly with a ram-rodded solution in hopes of making the problem just go away. If we remain reactionary, chances become very high that our quick resolution will cause another problem or swing the issue to another problematic extreme. If we implement reactionary measures, we will be busy chasing down issues that were exacerbated by our shoot-from-the-hip reactions. Stay urgent, yes. But let's keep our balance and give ourselves a chance to get that permanent resolution verified as efficiently as possible.

By taking this calm approach, we allow ourselves to get into a surgical mindset that can confirm the certainties of the problem and move our investigation forward to get to the root of the issue. We *will not be able to be surgical if we are reactionary*. A blanket resolution will produce blanket, unanticipated results. But a surgical resolution can be monitored, controlled, and assessed with more focus and accuracy. Stay balanced, assess the impact accurately, and navigate from temporary mitigation to permanent resolution.

You, your team and your constituents will be grateful that you took this route in your troubleshooting process. Applying solutions surgically will prevent issues from returning to your to-do list!

It's best not to apply this principle to an unnecessary extreme. We must avoid trying to resolve the issue at the minutest detail. If we go this route, we risk not actually resolving it and getting frustrated at the numerous failed attempts. It's all about getting a sense for how the technology works. We need to get familiar with the relevant tools for the technology we are trying to fix. Learn how to resolve an issue with a resolution that goes fully as far as the root of the problem, but no further. Avoiding collateral damage is always a best practice! After all, we want permanent resolutions without any unwanted side effects. The proof of our effectiveness is whether we resolve problems without creating new ones. Gaining a greater feel for how the technology works and its applicable tools will help you apply surgical resolutions that solve problems permanently.

The added benefit of resolving problems surgically is that we give ourselves time to understand exactly *why* the resolution worked. This is an important part of our pursuit of certainty. When we resolve surgically, we gain a much more concrete understanding of what the root problem was, why it was happening, and how exactly our resolution solved the problem. Let's hold ourselves to this higher standard of troubleshooting. People will notice that our resolutions are permanent. Our diligent work will reward us. Keep learning, keep going, and remain persistent in your surgical mindset.

If a whole IT team in an organization takes a surgical approach to troubleshooting, they will start to pivot from being reactive to being preventative. Ask almost any IT manager; a team that operates preventatively instead of reactively is preferred! A team that attacks issues from a preventative posture operates from a position of strength. Being preventative proves that we are harnessing and staying on top of the technology as a team instead of the technology controlling us. By being surgical, we ensure that we control our controllables and remain in command of the technology as much as possible. We don't want to get outflanked because a half-baked solution landed with unwanted impact and now we are back to being reactive again. This is why being surgical is so important. By being surgical we maintain our position of strength and remain in a preventative stance. By staying surgical we maintain a firm grasp on the reins of our technology so that we can harness it on behalf of the business.

MINDSET PRINCIPLE #7: REDEFINE YOUR SATISFACTION AND SUCCESS

Maybe you are someone who finds satisfaction in your work by getting a long list of to-do's checked off the list. Or maybe you get satisfaction out of rarely failing, making the hard accomplishments seem simple. Or perhaps you consider yourself successful when you get through a project and bring it to completion with seemingly few setbacks.

Regardless of how you have gained satisfaction from your work in the past, feeling successful and finding satisfaction in your new tech career will occur differently than in any other field. For example, if you get satisfaction from seeing the physical outcome of a finished product, you likely will not receive the same satisfaction in IT.

Quite a bit of IT is virtual—it's evidences are mostly displayed on a screen and within a device. We cannot expect to gain satisfaction in the same way as we did in a previous industry. We cannot expect to forklift our satisfaction or definition of success into IT and expect it to operate the same way for us. How we seek satisfaction in our work will need to be modified in order to feel successful in IT.

One of the primary reasons why we will need to adjust our definition of success is that achievement in IT is not always simple and straightforward. Fixing complicated technologies requires navigating through some complex variables and obstacles. The problems you had to solve in your past job may not have been as significant or urgent as they are in IT. Success and satisfaction typically come only after a lot of hard work in IT. That list of to-do's in IT can sometimes take much longer to accomplish than we expect because fixing things is not always not simple or straightforward. But if we patiently endure and follow through to achieve real solutions, we will succeed and enjoy satisfaction.

There are always many obstacles, plenty of things to do, and lots of failed attempts as we troubleshoot and learn each day. The progress we make and experiential knowledge that we gain in IT is always hard-earned. It is never given. We might not even realize that we have these expectations, definitions of success, and preconceived notions of satisfaction from our previous work or school experiences. That's okay, it's normal. These notions and definitions were subconsciously formed by our past habits and work experiences. But it is best to get prepared *now* not only for the challenges but also the change required. Our mindset will need to be modified to redefine our success and satisfaction too.

To redefine our satisfaction and success, we must allow these expectations of success and satisfaction to morph. If we hold tightly to our previous expectations, we will be disappointed when we don't feel success and satisfaction in all the previous ways. Maybe you are looking to overcome obstacles quickly to feel successful, but the obstacles aren't giving way so quickly in IT. Early successes, even small ones, may not happen as frequently as you would like. Or maybe you are looking for a quick victory over a to-do list, but the progress through it is taking much longer than you anticipated in IT. Maybe the string of failed attempts while troubleshooting is disheartening. Unfortunately, this could lead to feelings of greater discouragement. If you respond to this adversity by concluding too quickly that you are not good at IT, this discouragement could trigger a downward spiral in your confidence and mental fortitude.

To redefine your success and satisfaction, be kind to yourself by allowing yourself plenty of time to acclimate. Use the helpful mindset principles in this book to respond to the challenges. Allow 500-1,000 days to get your confidence up and get comfortable in your new career. Be patient with yourself. Celebrate each problem ticket you resolve and each tech concept you learn.

A very strong indicator of success in IT is the experiential knowledge we gain. The challenge of applying our knowledge in the most effective way will always be there. But that deep, detailed knowledge is what we should be after, and when we gain it we should allow ourselves to feel successful and take satisfaction from having gained it.

Focus on the technologies and become sensitive to those details instead of focusing on your own perceived limits. Lose sight of yourself and be enamored with the awesome capabilities of the technologies, and pursue with curiosity the understanding you seek. Control what you can control—your attitude, your effort, and your care for accomplishing and solving problems thoroughly.

Avoid belittling yourself for your shortcomings, or self-consciously cutting yourself down for little failures or misunderstandings. Keep learning, keep moving forward, and at the next opportunity prove to yourself that you've learned to apply your experiential knowledge more effectively. Don't sweat the small stuff.

Another important way to redefine your success and satisfaction is to celebrate your daily successes, even if you are successfully fixing only smaller things. Document in your personal notes the details of what you learned and how you fixed something so that you can use it quickly again next time. Give yourself mental kudos when you overcome an obstacle. Encourage yourself with positive self-talk when your troubleshooting revealed an important clue. Just because you haven't solved the issue yet doesn't mean you're not on your way. Just because you haven't fixed something yet and you are in the middle of the troubleshooting process doesn't mean you won't get there. You'll get there. And when you get there, and you figure it out and fix it . . . it *feels good.*

Success and satisfaction in IT come from staying steadfast and remaining persistent. They come by staying in attack mode and ready to overcome the next obstacle. You will gain success by being resourceful and pulling your weight while working with your team. You will find success by finding a new angle to get at the problem's source, by accepting the daily grind and attacking new challenges with heart and grit. This is the soil in which success and satisfaction grow. Grow where you're planted and just... keep... going. Your mind is a muscle. Continue to exercise that mental muscle. Give yourself a chance to keep going, keep working, keep developing and keep discovering.

Here's to you and your pursuit—not of perfection—but of real, hard-earned *satisfaction.*

MINDSET PRINCIPLE #8: LET TECHNOLOGY INFLUENCE YOU, ALL THE TIME

When we are just starting out or are relatively new to the tech space, our minds are in the process of adjusting to how different technologies operate. As we try to understand and fix them, we are navigating a narrow road. We will be tempted to trail off into either of two extremes. These two extremes are like ditches on either side of this narrow road. This narrow road leads to technological excellence, and we can stay on this road and avoid the ditches on either side only by maintaining a humble, curious, and persistent mindset. But maintaining this mindset isn't always so easy, and these ditches are hazardous.

The first ditch is a mindset in which we

start viewing ourselves as already quite skilled and accomplished. We have attained some success, and we have grown. This is true. We may have mastered a certain technology. But let's be wary that this sense of accomplishment and know-how does not become the foundation for over-confidence.

Over-confidence comes from thinking our success in one technology or situation will automatically lead to success in another scenario. True, the mindset and skills generally are transferrable. But our minds want to think that because we know about one technology, we now know quite a bit about technology in general. Our minds want to think this way because self-awareness isn't necessarily our forte, especially when we experience early success but haven't faced larger obstacles or more complex problems. When major obstacles do come, then we're failing to fix something and "it wasn't this difficult or messed up last time."

Over-confidence will lead us to overlook important details that end up inhibiting our ability to actualize a solution. The problem is, technology wants to be understood deeply, in all its awesome details. When we are over-confident, our configuration and solutions are inevitably incomplete and unsound because we've missed integral parts of the problem and major aspects of the technology's functionality. It is easy to over-simplify the technology and over-amplify our abilities. And when our solution lands, it isn't functional. Ugh! Don't stay stuck in this rut. Get back onto the trail of humility, curiosity and persistence quickly.

The second ditch comes from viewing technology problems as though we must wrestle them into submission. We could call this the Fix it by Force ditch. If we fall into this ditch, we are persistent. But curious for the details? Mentally humble as we approach the problem?--not so much. When we trail off into this ditch, our tactic becomes enforcing our configuration and dominating the technology because we think we have to force it to work. The problem is that technology isn't to be wrestled or dominated into submission. It just doesn't work that way. Don't stay stuck in this rut either.

In order to stay on the narrow road of humility, curiosity, and persistence, we have to believe that technology *wants to be understood.* It wants to be formed and fashioned *with* its grain, not *against* its grain. And for us to understand it, we need to let it impress itself upon us. We need to take it all in rather than trying to take it on in a contest of wills. If we continue in this ditch and approach the technology with force, we'll break more than just that technology. We could break some other functionalities it touches and other business processes, creating an even bigger problem. Taking this approach and staying in the Fix it by Force ditch also weakens our stamina. We end up prolonging our own frustration. And other people's frustrations will rise too. If we stay in this ditch, we'll end up fixating on the problem rather than accounting for exactly what it is telling us.

Regardless of which ditch we may fall into most, the solution is simple and the same. Stay humble. Stay curious. Stay persistent. These may not be easy to implement, but if we keep these mindset principles handy we'll begin to start implementing them as we recognize the ditches for what they are. Maintaining these mindset principles will help us stay productive and avoid unnecessary frustration. They will help us avoid both ditches and navigate our way through our tech career more smoothly.

Let's allow the technology to make its impression on us by staying humble and curious. Let's study it, listen to it, and let its behavior speak. We're not technology enforcers. We are painter-puzzlers and scientific artisans of technology. Avoid falling into either ditch by staying humble and remaining curious. Keep focusing on how to work *with* the technology instead of as one who must work against it. Don't disregard its nature or try to force it into submission. The technology is going to do what it was built to do. Listen, learn, and stay mentally nimble.

Remain humble, curious, and persistent. Put into practice the mindset principles we discussed. Organize them in your mental toolbox, and keep them ready. Always be ready to modify your mindset as you move forward. And keep this handbook handy.